PETS TO THE RESCUE

Tara and Tiree, Fearless Friends
A True Story

First Aladdin Paperbacks edition August 2003

ALADDIN PAPERBACKS
An imprint of Simon & Schuster
Children's Publishing Division
1230 Avenue of the Americas
New York, NY 10020

Book design by Sammy Yuen Jr.
The text of this book was set in Times New Roman.
The illustrations are rendered in watercolor.

Printed in the United States of America
10 9

Also available in a Simon & Schuster Books for Young Readers
hardcover edition.

The Library of Congress has cataloged the hardcover edition as follows:
Clements, Andrew, 1949–
Tara and Tiree, fearless friends: a true story / by Andrew Clements ;
illustrated by Ellen Beier.
p. cm. (Pets to the rescue)
Summary: When Jim falls through the ice on a lake in Canada,
his two dogs try to rescue him.
ISBN 0-689-82917-5 (hc)
[1. Dogs—Fiction. 2. Rescues—Fiction. 3. Pets—Fiction.
4. Canada—Fiction.] I. Beier, Ellen, ill. II. Title. III. Series
PZ7.C59118 Tar 2002 [E]-dc21 2001057666ISBN 0-689-82917-5 (hc)
ISBN-13: 978-0-689-83441-7 (Aladdin pbk.)
ISBN-10: 0-689-83441-1 (Aladdin pbk.)
1210 LAK

PETS TO THE RESCUE

Tara and Tiree, Fearless Friends

A True Story

Written by Andrew Clements
Illustrated by Ellen Beier

Ready-to-Read
Aladdin Paperbacks

New York   London   Toronto   Sydney   Singapore

4

When Jim was a boy in Canada,
his family had dogs.
Jim loved those dogs.
They were like part of
his family.

When Jim grew up,
he still loved dogs.
He learned how to train them.
He helped dogs learn
to be good.

He always said, "There is
no such thing as a bad dog."
Training dogs became Jim's job.

Jim had two dogs named Tara
and Tiree.

Tara was mostly black.
Tiree was mostly gold.
Jim loved them both,
and they loved him, too.
Jim and his dogs liked
the wintertime.

They had good coats
to keep warm.
They played in the snow.
They went for long walks.

10

They liked going out,
but they liked going back in, too.
It was good to sit by the fire
and listen to the wind.

Jim's house was by a lake.
Every winter there was ice on it.

One day Jim went for a walk
out on the lake.
Tara and Tiree went too.
The dogs loved to run
across the ice.

It was very cold.
Jim was ready to go back home.
Then all at once the ice broke.

14

Jim fell into the cold,
cold water.

Jim called for help.
No one was near.
No one could hear him.

But Tara and Tiree heard Jim
and came running.
Jim wanted the dogs
to stay away.
He was afraid for them.

But Tiree loved Jim.
She wanted to help.

When she came near the hole,
the ice broke again.
Tiree fell into the water
with Jim.

The water was so cold.
Jim knew he did not have
much time.

Jim tried to help Tiree get out.
But the ice broke
more and more.

Jim hoped Tara would run away.
He did not want her to fall
in the water too.
But Tara did not run away.
She wanted to help.

First Tara got down low.
Then she came closer,
little by little.
The ice did not break.

Jim put out his hand.
Tara got very close.
Then Jim got hold of
Tara's collar.

Jim held on.
Tara pulled back, but Jim was
too big.
He was still in the cold water.

Then Tiree did something
very smart.
She walked on Jim's back—
up and out of the water!

Tiree was cold,
but she was safe!
Did she run off the ice?
No. She loved Jim too much
to run away.

Tiree got down on her belly
like Tara.
She got close to Jim.
Jim held out his other hand.
And he grabbed on to Tiree's
collar!

The two dogs pulled back hard.
They slipped, but they didn't
stop.
Slowly they pulled Jim up
onto the ice.
He was safe.

Tara and Tiree had saved
his life!
Soon they were all back
in the house.

They sat by the fire
until they were warm again.

Jim always said, "There is
no such thing as a bad dog."
Now Jim says something else,
too:

"There *is* such a thing as a
    brave and wonderful dog!"

Jim is sure of this,
because he has two of them—
Tara and Tiree.